Spotlight on
Kids Can Code

Coding for
DIGITAL SECURITY

Patricia Harris

PowerKiDS press
New York

Published in 2018 by The Rosen Publishing Group, Inc.
29 East 21st Street, New York, NY 10010

Copyright © 2018 by The Rosen Publishing Group, Inc.

All rights reserved. No part of this book may be reproduced in any form without permission in writing from the publisher, except by a reviewer.

First Edition

Editor: Melissa Raé Shofner
Book Design: Michael J. Flynn
Interior Layout: Rachel Rising

Photo Credits: Cover Adrian Weinbrecht/Cultura/Getty Images; pp. 1, 3–24 (coding background) Lukas Rs/Shutterstock.com; p. 4 Albachiaraa/Shutterstock.com; p. 5 Hiya Images/Corbis/Getty Images; p. 7 Monkey Business Images/Shutterstock.com; p. 9 © iStockphoto.com/visualspace; p. 10 frank_peters/Shutterstock.com; p. 12 Scanrail1/Shutterstock.com; p.13 Anna_leni/Shutterstock.com;p. 15 China Photos/Getty Images News/Getty Images; p. 17 MaeManee/Shutterstock.com; p. 18 Georgejmclittle/Shutterstock.com; p. 21 Photon photo/Shutterstock.com.

Cataloging-in-Publication Data
Names: Harris, Patricia.
Title: Coding for digital security / Patricia Harris.
Description: New York : PowerKids Press, 2018. | Series: Spotlight on kids can code | Includes index.
Identifiers: ISBN 9781508155270 (pbk.) | ISBN 9781508155164 (library bound) | ISBN 9781508154815 (6 pack)
Subjects: LCSH: Computer security–Juvenile literature. | Information technology–Security measures–Juvenile literature. | Digital media–Security measures–Juvenile literature. | Data protection–Juvenile literature.
Classification: LCC QA76.9.A25 H37 2018 | DDC 005.8-dc23

Manufactured in the United States of America

CPSIA Compliance Information: Batch #BS17PK: For Further Information contact Rosen Publishing, New York, New York at 1-800-237-9932

Contents

Stop, Thief!..................................4
Avoiding Identity Theft................8
Cybercrimes...............................10
Internet of Things.....................12
Software Piracy.........................14
Digital Defenders......................16
Protecting Companies and
    the Government....................20
A Growing Problem...................22
Glossary.....................................23
Index..24
Websites....................................24

Stop, Thief!

Bank robberies may seem like things of the past, but they still happen. Fortunately, banks take steps to keep customers, workers, and money safe. If a robbery occurs, security guards and police officers are usually able to track down the thieves and return the stolen money to the bank. However, there's another kind of robbery that can be harder to stop—digital robbery.

Jay got a new cell phone for his birthday. He added his favorite **apps**, his contacts, and personal information about himself. His parents even let him add an app that stores his credit card information and allows him to pay for things using his phone. Then, at a clothing store, Jay set his cell phone down while looking at some new jeans. When he turned back around, his phone was gone. Jay really needed digital security now.

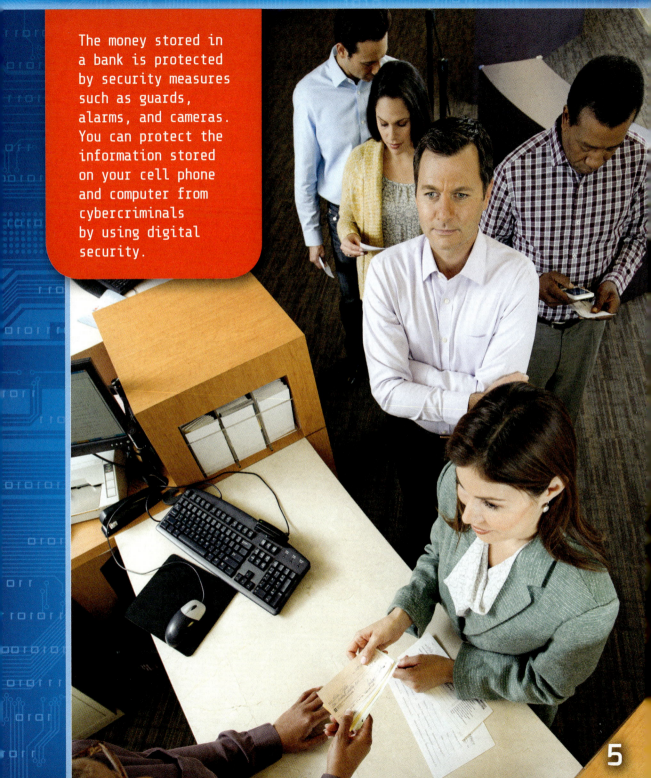

The money stored in a bank is protected by security measures such as guards, alarms, and cameras. You can protect the information stored on your cell phone and computer from cybercriminals by using digital security.

It was a good thing Jay was aware of the digital security measures that could be used on his cell phone. For instance, he set up his phone so that it required a four-digit key to be unlocked. He also stored his personal data and passwords in a secure app that required extra passwords to access. His credit card app needed a fingerprint to work. Jay knew how to protect his **identity** from being stolen from his phone.

Jay immediately talked to the clothing store's security guard. He borrowed an employee's smartphone and used an app designed to find other cell phones. The app showed that his phone was still in the store. The security guard found Jay's stolen phone on the floor near the bathrooms.

Breaking the Code

Digital security is how you protect your online identity. However, no digital security system is perfect. Cybercriminals steal many people's identities each year. This isn't just because those people lost an unprotected phone. Identities may also be stolen using data stolen from online databases maintained by companies and social networking sites.

The person who stole Jay's phone may have gotten away, but Jay's online identity was safe.

Avoiding Identity Theft

It's important to learn about digital security because the crimes surrounding our online lives are not going away. Jay's stolen cell phone could have led to identity theft, which is the illegal use of someone's personal information. A thief may then pretend to be that person, usually to steal money or information. Stealing someone's wallet or purse may also lead to identity theft.

Today, online criminals have developed numerous ways to collect information from you. Phishing **scams**—and the related vishing and smishing scams—are common ways online scammers find out your personal information. If you're asked for personal information in an e-mail, phone call, or text message, don't give it out. Even if you think you know the sender, check with them and ask why they need this information.

Breaking the Code

Phishing is the practice of using e-mail to get personal information from other people. Phishers send e-mails asking for information with the hope that victims will respond. When similar requests are made over the phone, it's called vishing. In a text message, it's called smishing.

Phishing e-mails often look like they're from trusted websites. Double check to be sure you know who is asking for your information before you respond.

Cybercrimes

Digital crimes, often called cybercrimes, include pharming and **hacking**. Pharming is using malware to send users to a fake website without the user's knowledge. Malware is **software** installed, or put in place, on someone's computer by a cybercriminal. Personal information, such as credit card numbers, entered on the fake site may be collected by cybercriminals.

Cybercriminals may also hack into business or government databases to steal passwords. Stolen passwords are then used to steal even more information. In a denial of service (DoS) attack, a hacker uses a computer and Internet connection to send many information requests to a target. A targeted company's systems may overload and not be able to serve the needs of real customers. The systems may even stop working entirely.

A distributed denial of service attack (DDoS) is a type of DoS attack that uses hundreds and even thousands of computers and Internet connections to stage an attack on a target. This often requires **botnets**. The huge number of information requests from different computers is like a crowd of people trying to squeeze through a small doorway at the same time.

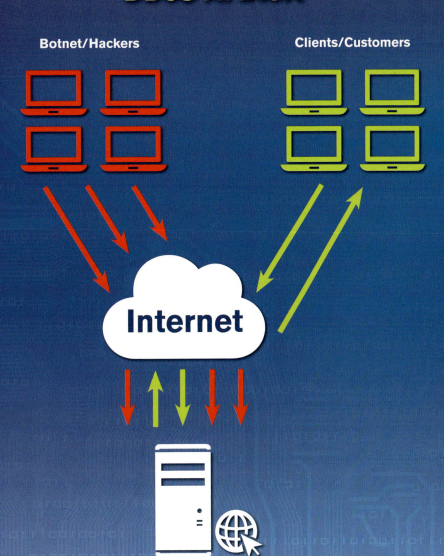

DDoS ATTACK

Internet of Things

Many different products use computer **technology** today. Cars use many kinds of computers. Some cars are equipped with **GPS** systems and computers that can call for help if the driver has an accident. You can even buy refrigerators with computers installed in them. Other products that can send and receive data through the Internet include home security systems, watches, and running shoes. This ever-growing network of computers and devices is called the "Internet of things."

Recently, cybercriminals have begun using the Internet of things for DDoS attacks. Cybercriminals use Internet-connected devices, such as DVRs and smart TVs, to create a botnet for their attack. Internet of things products are often left open to these types of attacks because people don't think to use cybersecurity measures on them.

In October 2016, a botnet called "Mirai" targeted Internet of things devices and turned them into bots that helped spread a huge cyberattack. This attack brought down many popular websites, including Twitter, Spotify, and Amazon.

INTERNET OF THINGS

Software Piracy

Software piracy is the use or reproduction of someone else's software without their consent. Expensive computer software can be illegally copied and sold as the real thing. If you find low-priced software, you may think you're getting a great deal. However, you may actually be buying illegal fake software.

Be aware that software piracy can cause problems for consumers as well as sellers and creators. Using pirated software could get you into trouble with the law. It may also harm your computer by introducing malware. **Updating** pirated software may cause it to stop working. Pirated software also leaves users open to cyberattacks because it's often less secure than the original software.

Breaking the Code

Software piracy is no small crime. It costs developers in the United States more than $10 billion in lost earnings each year. In 2014, approximately 61 percent of the software being used in central and eastern Europe was illegal. The amount of pirated software being used in some Asian markets is around 90 percent!

Software piracy is more common in countries where it's hard for people to buy or download legal software. When police find out about a piracy operation, they seize the illegal software and destroy it.

Digital Defenders

Digital security is the responsibility of companies, but it's your responsibility, too. When using digital devices such as computers and smartphones, you leave behind information that's collected by the companies whose services you use. Service providers, sellers, and other companies use that data to improve their businesses. Profiles are created to let other companies share information about you. Unfortunately, cybercriminals might access that information. If they discover your e-mail address, they might send you an e-mail that contains malware. It might include information from sites you visit online to draw your attention.

There are steps you can take to protect yourself from cybercriminals. Use your Wi-Fi and **geolocation** devices wisely. Check your privacy settings on social networking sites. Avoid websites that don't appear safe or reliable.

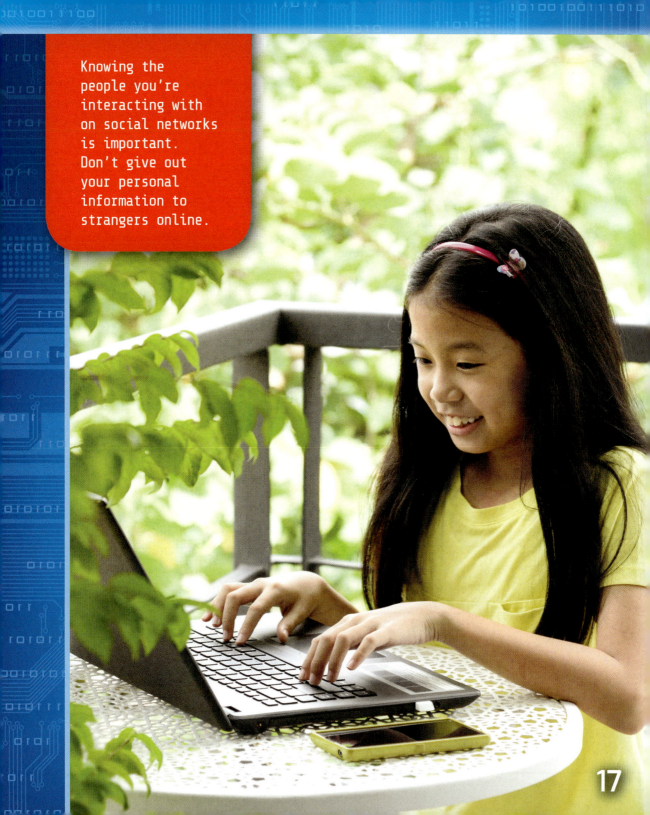

Knowing the people you're interacting with on social networks is important. Don't give out your personal information to strangers online.

When it comes to digital security, you can start by using passwords wisely. You should never share your passwords with friends. Don't store your passwords in a school notebook or in an app that's not password protected. Use password manager software to store them. Strong passwords have at least eight characters that include capital letters, lowercase letters, numbers, and symbols. Don't use a single word from the dictionary, and don't reuse passwords.

Keeping your computer software and apps up to date helps protect you, too. Updates are often written in response to possible security problems. You can also use security tools to check your e-mail and downloaded files. These tools include antivirus software and malware-removal software.

A strong password is an important security measure everyone can use.

BAD PASSWORDS	BETTER PASSWORDS	EXCELLENT PASSWORDS
kitty	1Kitty	1Ki77y725
susan	Susan53	.SuSaN5335
jellyfish	jelly22fish	Je11y22fi$h
ilovepizza	!LovePizza	!Lov3Pi22a88
samsmith	$am.smith	Z2m/Zm1tt
123abc	cba321	ayz.32.xbz
doglover	Dog.lov3r	dOG.lov3r

Protecting Companies and the Government

Digital security is an added cost for companies, but cyberattacks can also cost them money. Businesses can lose customers when information is stolen from their systems. They lose sales when their systems are hit with DDoS attacks. The cost to the government can also be high, especially when cybercriminals attack national security sites.

One way to improve digital security is encryption of data. Encryption is a way to turn information (or data) that anyone can read into information (or data) that must be unlocked with a key, or special code. A system may use one of many encryption **algorithms** to change plain data into encrypted data. You may see "https://" before a website address. The "s" stands for "secure," and that means the data has been encrypted.

RSA is a popular data-encryption program. RSA uses two prime numbers, each 100 digits long, to mix up data and make it unreadable to anyone without the key.

21

A Growing Problem

Even if computer users—individuals, companies, and governments—follow all security measures, they may still fall victim to a cyberattack. Unfortunately, it's becoming increasingly difficult to provide effective digital security. There are several reasons for this:

- The Internet is being used more and more. People are buying and selling goods, connecting with friends and business associates, storing medical records, handling banking, seeking information, and doing many other tasks online.
- Smartphones have introduced a new point of access for cybercriminals, who steal phones or hack into the phone system.
- Some companies look for security entry points and sell them, sometimes to people who use them for illegal purposes.
- Cyberattacks on businesses are on the rise. Often they're attacks by people outside a business, but sometimes they're attacks by people who work within a company.
- Computers are becoming faster and that helps everyone work faster, including cybercriminals.

If you think you've been the victim of a cyberattack, take action quickly.

Glossary

algorithm: A set of steps that are followed in order to solve a mathematical problem or complete a computer process.

application (app): A program that performs one of the tasks for which a computer, smartphone, or tablet is used.

botnet: A network of computers that have been connected together by malware.

geolocation: The process of finding the location of a person or device using information found online.

GPS: A navigating system that uses satellite signals to tell the user where they are and direct them to a destination. Short for global positioning system.

hack: To use a computer to gain unapproved access to data in a system.

identity: Who a person is, including their personal information, bank account numbers, passwords, and more.

scam: A scheme in which someone is deceived, usually done to get money from the target.

software: A program that runs on a computer and performs certain functions.

technology: A method that uses science to solve problems and the tools used to solve those problems.

update: To install the latest version of a program on a computer.

Index

A
algorithm, 20
Amazon, 13
apps, 4, 6, 18

B
botnet, 11, 12, 13

D
denial of service (DoS) attack, 10, 11
distributed denial of service (DDos) attack, 11, 12, 20

E
encryption, 20, 21

G
geolocation, 16
GPS, 12

H
hacking, 10

I
identity, 6, 7, 8
Internet of things, 12, 13

M
malware, 10, 14, 16, 18
Mirai, 13

P
passwords, 6, 10, 18, 19
pharming, 10
phishing, 8, 9

R
RSA, 21

S
smishing, 8
software piracy, 14, 15
Spotify, 13

T
Twitter, 13

V
vishing, 8

W
Wi-Fi, 16

Websites

Due to the changing nature of Internet links, PowerKids Press has developed an online list of websites related to the subject of this book. This site is updated regularly. Please use this link to access the list: www.powerkidslinks.com/skcc/cds